THE LITTLE BOOK OF

ANGELS

THE LITTLE BOOK OF

ANGELS

Nicole Masson

CHRONICLE BOOKS

SAN FRANCISCO

First published in the United States of America in 2013 by
Chronicle Books LLC.

First published in 2011 by Éditions du Chêne—Hachette Livre.

Library of Congress Cataloguing-in-Publication Data available.

ISBN 978-1-4521-1441-5

Manufactured in China

Designed by Hillary Caudle
Translated by Elizabeth Bell

The images published in this book belong to the private collection of
Albert Van den Bosch (www.collectomania.be) with the exception
of the following pages: © Leemage: pages 17 (© Costa/Leemage); 27,
151, 157 (© Selva/Leemage); 31, 67, 71, 73, 77, 79, 85, 91, 129, 131, 133, 165,
167 (© Fototeca/Leemage); 65 (© Bianchetti/Leemage); 81 (© Abecasis/
Leemage). © Kharbine-Tapabor: pages 39, 45, 61, 103, 141, 143, 145, 147;
pages 33, 119, 127 (© coll. IM/Kharbine-Tapabor); 105, 107 (© Jewish
Memories/Kharbine-Tapabor). © DR: page 131.

10 9 8 7 6 5 4 3 2 1

Chronicle Books LLC
680 Second Street
San Francisco, California 94107
www.chroniclebooks.com

CONTENTS

Je voudrais à la place de clous et d'une couronne d'épines pour le Sacré Cœur, une couronne formée du cœur de tous les hommes.

S. François de Sales.

In place of nails and a crown of thorns for the Sacred Heart, I wish a crown formed of the hearts of all men. —ST. FRANCIS DE SALES

✷ ANGELS, ENIGMATIC BEINGS ✷

The invention of color lithography in 1837 by Frenchman Godefroy Engelmann enabled the widespread distribution of pious images. The popular new chromolithographs, in France called simply "*chromos*," often commemorated First Communion in the Catholic religion, when it was customary to give out missals or images to the faithful. They served many secular purposes as well, such as promoting department stores, small businesses, and industries amidst early fascination with the new means of communication.

This little book gathers together a gallery of angels that appeared in the early mass-distributed *chromos*, and accompanies them with text including history, musings, and verse to present an overview of these enigmatic celestial beings in earlier times rejected by the Church, which viewed the anthropomorphic figures of light as potential rivals of Jesus Christ and feared a drift toward paganism.

Despite such hindrances, angels became universal; they are found not only in Judeo-Christian culture but also in Islam and folk beliefs. The Bible alludes to them in both the Old and New Testaments, and the Apocrypha texts—so called because they are not officially sanctioned by all persuasions—enter into detail on their appearance, actions, and functions. Perhaps most precise are the renderings of angels found in the "intertestamental" books, those written in the period between the two Testaments, such as the Book of Enoch (great-grandfather of Noah; a canon of the Old Testament in the Ethiopian Orthodox

Heureuse l'âme qui, après avoir
été docile aux conseils de son Ange
gardien, sera conduite par lui au ciel.

S. Louis de Gonzague.

MAISON BOUASSE-LEBEL ... Lecène & Cⁱᵉ   5654   PARIS.

*Happy the soul who obeys the counsel of one's guardian angel, and
is conducted by him unto heaven.* —**ST. LOUIS DE GONZEAGUE**

Church) or some of the Apocalypses. These Revelations (the original meaning of "apocalypse") highlight angelic interventions and give meticulous descriptions of the "celestial hierarchy." Protectors, messengers of God, permitting humans to communicate with the invisible, endowed with majestic wings to navigate between heaven and earth, angels are fascinating in all religions.

Representation of angels owes much to the small, winged divinities of ancient Mesopotamia and later influences from the Greco-Roman pantheon. The best-known angels are the three archangels shared by the monotheistic religions, Gabriel, Raphael, and Michael; the most common are guardian angels, who serve as companions in the daily life of humans and stand vigil as they sleep. The Angel of the Lord, cherubim with their blue wings, fiery seraphim . . . such holy angels can be "elected" protectors of a nation or a people, and each accomplishes a specific mission, such as patrons of travelers, pharmacists, pastry chefs, even radio and television workers. Their supernatural powers have always fascinated humans, who project upon angels their own fears and hopes.

"DE CONSIDERATIONE"
BERNARD DE CLAIRVAUX (1090–1153)

"Angels are powerful, glorious, blessed, of distinct personalities, divided in rank according to their worthiness, faithful to the order given them from the beginning, perfect in their nature, ethereal in body, immortal and passionless, not created thus, but made thus through grace, not by nature; beings pure in mind, benign in will, devoted to God, wholly chaste, unanimous in harmony, secure in peace, God's creation dedicated to the praise and service of the divine."

WHERE DO ANGELS COME FROM?

The word "angel" comes from the Latin *angelus*, a transcription from the Greek *aggelos* (αγγελος), meaning "messenger."

If there are angels in the text of the Bible, originally written in Hebrew, why is the word Greek? The first Greek version of the Bible is called the Septuagint Bible, which is acknowledged as sacred because the seventy assembled Elders were said to have each produced the exact same translation independently of one another. From there, *aggelos* came into use in scriptural translations for the Hebrew word for "messenger," *mal'akh*, the base of which means "to send," understood as "sent from God."

In the Old Testament, the designation "messenger" may apply to prophets or preachers. "Angels" are distinctly defined first and foremost by their function: they come from heaven to visit humankind and announce the intentions of the divine.

Comparative religion studies show the belief in the existence of beings who play an intermediary role between limited, mortal humans and an all-powerful divinity all around the world. The religions of the Book are no different. They share a Bible, and angels are found in Jewish tradition and in Islam as well as in Christianity.

THE CREATURES OF BABYLON

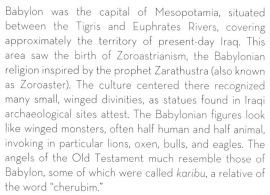

Babylon was the capital of Mesopotamia, situated between the Tigris and Euphrates Rivers, covering approximately the territory of present-day Iraq. This area saw the birth of Zoroastrianism, the Babylonian religion inspired by the prophet Zarathustra (also known as Zoroaster). The culture centered there recognized many small, winged divinities, as statues found in Iraqi archaeological sites attest. The Babylonian figures look like winged monsters, often half human and half animal, invoking in particular lions, oxen, bulls, and eagles. The angels of the Old Testament much resemble those of Babylon, some of which were called *karibu*, a relative of the word "cherubim."

We also see the concept of opposition between good and evil demigods, related to the Bible's fallen angels. The two cultures were mutually influential: twice, the Bible recounts, King Nebuchadnezzar II conquered the city of Jerusalem and banished from his capital thousands of Jews. They would not return until fifty years later, with the taking of Babylon by Cyrus, king of Persia, in 539 B.C.

HOW TO RECOGNIZE
AN ANGEL

The term "angel" is used to describe many celestial entities. Of these, the best known are the seraphim, cherubim, and archangels. Nowhere in the Old Testament is there a complete definition or list of all the attributes of angels, nor even a litany of their names or structure of their hierarchy. Treatises on angels come in books written a bit later, contested to different degrees among the monotheistic religions.

In the Bible, angels are presented as invisible beings who may suddenly appear to humans at God's orders. "Angels of light" with luminous bodies and radiant faces, dressed in white, they are said to emerge from a burst of light that dazzles the witnesses. Often encircled by fire, they can walk upon the flames. The intensity of their apparition is hard for common mortals to bear; an exception seems to be for pious women whose souls are at peace.

Angels are usually very large—physically, they are a far cry from cherubs!—and of human form, sometimes on horseback or even armed with an impressive sword and breastplate.

Large or small, angels' wings, which allow them to fly between heaven and earth, symbolize the intermediary nature of their character—beings of celestial origin and by nature "of the air," but who serve the function of messengers to earth. Thanks to their wings, they return very quickly to the skies, where they can see everything. They do not feed. They do not reproduce. They are immortal.

✴ ANGEL WINGS ✴

In sacred texts, angels are typically shown surrounded by a very bright white halo; cherubim in a deep blue that blends with heavenly azure; and the fiery seraphim are red like the flames they bear. Many pre-modern painters traditionally employed these three colors in rendering the wings of angels. One exception to the rule is Italian Baroque master Caravaggio, who painted angels with black wings. In his famous work *Saint Matthew and the Angel* (1602), the angel pictured unfurls inky wings that meld into the darkness. In *Rest on the Flight into Egypt* (c. 1597), a white-clad angel turns his back to the viewer, revealing highly realistic dark wings, like those of a pigeon or eagle; and in the provocative *Amor Vincit Omnia* (Love Conquers All) (1602), the same dusky bird wings are seen. The ambiguity in this manner of using white and black has been extensively debated, since the image of a black angel was long reserved for the fallen one, the demon.

Angels' beauty too is sometimes marked by ambiguity, with charms that may be either beneficial or fatal. Quite unlike the depictions cited above, where the definitive wings are modeled after realistic flyers, other iconic images of angels are given beautiful wings covered with eyes—in this case, the symbolism would seem to emphasize their perfect and boundless vision. By contrast, in the film *The Blue Angel*, Marlene Dietrich's character, Lola, is a singer in a notorious cabaret by the same name, and a classic femme fatale—here the symbolic angel's allure leads her lover downward to a tragic end.

THE CELESTIAL HIERARCHY

The Greek meaning of the word "hierarchy" is "sacred government." In the celestial hierarchy, there are nine angelic orders, composed into three ranks with three choirs each.

The first hierarchy is closest to God and includes, in descending order of perfection, *seraphim*, or divine "burning ones"; *cherubim*, who represent the fullness of knowledge; and *thrones*, who are the seat of God in His glory.

The middle hierarchy governs. In its top choir are the *dominations*, who take preeminence and transmit orders; then come the *virtues*, who carry them out; and lastly the *powers*, who remove obstacles and hold demons at bay.

The last hierarchy has limited functions. It consists of the *principalities*, who head provinces; *archangels*, who head communities and cities; and lastly, simply *angels*, who each guide one person.

In the fourth century, the list of seraphim and cherubim was added to the Old Testament. In the New Testament, there is talk of a myriad of angels, heavenly legions, cherubim, seraphim, and the archangels Michael, Raphael, and Gabriel. In other sacred Christian texts, classes of angels are mentioned (archangels, thrones, seigneuries or dominations, principalities or archons, authorities and virtues, powers), and their rank depends not on their power but on their proximity to God.

Le Dieu
des Anges
s'est fait
homme
pour que l'homme
se nourrisse
du pain
des Anges.

(St Augustin.)

Blanchard, Orléans.   Nᵒ 2097.

The God of the Angels was made man so that man might partake of the bread of Angels. —ST. AUGUSTINE

THE GUARDIANS OF THE SEVEN HEAVENS

Unofficial, or "intertestamental," texts arrange the legions of angels in their own fashion and attribute to them distinct functions and locales. Theories vary from one book to the next; the mystics rebuke, critique, and correct one another, with variations too endless to list. However, the basic notion of a heavenly hierarchy and organization around God took hold in the popular imagination, in painting, and in the thinking of the Fathers of the Church.

Although the numbers or details may differ, generally the celestial hierarchy is expressed geographically, by the placement of angels in the seven heavens, with the heavens occupying concentric spheres. There are a total of seventy-two heavenly kingdoms, and seven palaces in the seventh heaven—the very place where profane pleasures famously send us! And the entrance to each palace is guarded by angels.

All this may sound like anecdote or folklore, but it is also the basis for a mystical interpretation of ascension: a soul's journey consists of rising from one heaven to the next, relying on angels for its passage. To cross each threshold, protective seals must be presented and complex formulas pronounced. The archangels Michael, Raphael, Gabriel, and Uriel play a major role in this journey, conducting the initiate soul toward the divine chariot and throne of God.

CHERUBIM, CUPIDS, ANGELS OF LOVE

When we speak of angels, the first image that comes to mind is often that of the plump, smiling cherub, small in stature, with curly hair and chubby cheeks. Cherubim are almost always shown with a pair of wings; they may sometimes also be blindfolded or bear a quiver full of arrows. These are not religious angels but the fusion of several winged beings from different cultural traditions. Greco-Roman mythology counts numerous winged divinities, from gods in the Pantheon—such as Eros, Cupid (god of Love), and Mercury, with his winged feet—to allegorical figures such as Victory. Wings represent the ability to move swiftly and to rise into the sky, hence the mingling of the sacred and profane, the mythological and religious. Little love angels, cupids, and *putti* (Italian architectural elements depicting fleshy cherubs), for example, are not the messengers of God on earth but creatures associated with messages between people in love, or with the wounds of love and desire—far from any divine origin! This blend of sources is evident in the case of Saint Valentine. A martyr saint, Valentine, in his folk-legend persona, inspires those in love and guides them in the choice of a mate. On his feast day, nearly everywhere in the world, small presents or cards with images of cherubs and cupids are exchanged. The presence of a bow and arrow readily distinguishes the allegorical Love figure from a true angel.

Bonne année

Happy New Year

⊱ MISTRUST OF ANGELS ⊰

The religions of the Book are always wary of angel veneration, which has the potential to reintroduce a sort of polytheism.

The Fathers of the Church emphasize the uniqueness of the role of the Messiah, God's only Son sent to earth. Angels, who are also messengers, are subaltern entities obedient to Jesus Christ. They must never be accorded too important a place in worship, especially in the more popular practices of devotion.

It took no fewer than three Councils—in Nicea (325), Constantinople (381), and Chalcedon (451)—to determine the exact place of angels, reaffirming the mystery of the incarnation of Jesus, who is no mere archangel or prophet sent by God, but truly God incarnate, God become man.

THE SEX OF ANGELS

Today, the expression "arguing about the sex of angels" means wasting time in pointless argument. Originally, though, it was a quite literal activity—and the theological debates on the subject, especially in Byzantium but also among the Church Fathers, were indeed interminable.

Should we imagine angels of both sexes? Are they purely spiritual beings, and therefore completely asexual? What do biblical texts say on the question?

Judging from a passage in Genesis stating that some angels are traitors to God and also lovers to women, and that it is lustfulness that brings about their fall, one may assume angels are in fact gendered—in any case, a chief characteristic of fallen angels seems to be that they give free rein to their wildest desires. This alleged source of disorder was exploited in witchcraft trials starting in the Middle Ages and is alluded to in the trial of Joan of Arc. Incubi, who licentiously enter women's bodies, and succubi, who seduce and arouse men, are the archetypal rebel angels who have become demons to tempt humans.

☆ SEX AND PERFECTION ☆

In the Kabbalah, angels sometimes form perfect couples, and their reciprocal desire contributes to their strength. Thus the cherubim who bear the Ark of the Covenant are sometimes depicted facing one another in the union of love.

On the other hand, the Gospels clearly state that angels take neither wife nor husband and that, upon resurrection, humans likewise are not married. This distinguishes the condition of having gender from that of using it. By their nature, angels spontaneously practice the abstinence that is prescribed to humans who consecrate their lives to God.

Seraphim have three pairs of wings. One pair folds in front of them to hide their nudity and their bodies down to the feet; it becomes a sort of loincloth, lending them a modest, solemn, and rooted sacerdotal image appropriate to their elevated rank in the celestial hierarchy.

The influence of Platonism can be detected in this search for balance and transcendence. Socrates, in Plato's *Banquet*, explains that the perfect being is one composed of both masculine and feminine elements; humans have been divided in two, and the sexual part seeks its other half to reconstitute perfect unity. The angels in their perfection embody this total, asexual unity.

THE ANGEL OF GOD

Several times in the Bible, the Angel of God is mentioned, without further specifics. He receives reports from other angels sent to earth. His identity is often blended with that of the archangel Michael.

This angel is seen as God's closest servant, manifesting to humankind His will. As such, he often transmits extremely important messages. For example, it is he who announces the birth of Samson. And when Sara, wife of Abraham, expels her servant Agar, who has borne to the patriarch a son named Ishmael, the Angel of God appears to the weary, disheartened exile in the desert and foretells that her son shall have numerous descendants.

The Angel of God protects the prophets, consoles Zachariah in his visions, and can intercede on behalf of humans to avert punishments.

When Yahweh demanded of Abraham the supreme sacrifice of his only son, Isaac, to test his faith, it was the Angel of God who stayed his hand at the last moment: the intention was enough.

The Angel of God is closer to humans than to the divine. In all these episodes, he appears as the representative of God, serving as messenger, guide, or armed enforcer. He wages constant combat with Satan and thus saves the children of Israel. In the Gospel he is sometimes called "the Angel of the Lord."

"THE ANGEL"
WILLIAM BLAKE (1757–1827)

I Dreamt a Dream! what can it mean?
And that I was a maiden Queen:
Guarded by an Angel mild:
Witless woe, was ne'er beguil'd!

And I wept both night and day
And he wip'd my tears away
And I wept both day and night
And hid from him my heart's delight.

So he took his wings and fled:
Then the morn blush'd rosy red:
I dried my tears & armed my fears,
With ten thousand shields and spears.

Soon my Angel came again;
I was arm'd, he came in vain:
For the time of youth was fled
And grey hairs were on my head.

WHO ARE THE CHERUBIM?

The name "cherubim" came from the Hebrew *keroub* (plural *keroubim*), which itself came from *karibu*, a word of Babylonian origin meaning "a second-rank deity having wings." In Eastern religion they are monsters, part human and part animal—usually with elements of lion or bull—who stand at the entrance to palaces, towns, and temples, their heads facing the visitor. The cherubim of the Bible retain this function: they are guardians who protect holy sites. That is why, after Adam and Eve were banished from their earthly paradise, cherubim were posted to guard the Tree of Life with their swirling swords. In another function, they are the guardians of the Ark of the Covenant, the wooden coffer containing the Tablets of the Law. The wings of two cherubim form a shelter that protects it. They cluster around the heavenly chariot as they transport it, and support the divine throne from beneath.

Cherubim are classed in the first ranks of the celestial hierarchy, above or below the seraphim, depending on the commentator. They stand for the fullness of knowledge. According to Saint Paul, the fullness of faith is love; that may be why the cherubim are aligned with the little love angels of antiquity.

WHAT DO CHERUBIM LOOK LIKE?

The representation of cherubs has evolved quite a bit over time and in different texts. The Bible usually describes them as monsters resembling griffins—half human, half beast—with several pairs of wings and several faces, and blue like the sky.

In the Book of Ezekiel, their vigilance is symbolized by numerous eyes: "And their whole body, and their backs, and their hands, and their wings are full of eyes round about." Hence, thanks to them, nothing escapes God.

Although they are most often blue, matching the sky, they are sometimes depicted, like seraphim, as red, signifying that they are inflamed with the love of God. In the past, a person who blushed was said to "turn as red as a cherub."

From the Renaissance onward, cherubs have been largely, and simply, represented as the face of a plump-cheeked infant, framed by two wings. Figures like these often adorn the keystones of churches, or the front of greeting cards.

In the Kabbalah, cherubim are rendered in "the color of the sun" and are said to be made up of ether; the gemstone associated with them is the amber-colored topaz, endowed with magical power and symbolizing justice.

CHERUBIM AND THE DIVINE CHARIOT

The Book of Ezekiel gives us the most details about cherubim and the divine chariot. Ezekiel, a prophet in exile in Babylon, bestows his visions upon the people of Israel in an astonishing outpouring of complex and wondrous details.

The cherubim form the throne of God, and in the heavenly chariot, they serve in place of wheels. They are driven by Spirit; they do not turn. Their motion is evidence of divine majesty. God, like the Eastern divinities, is thus endowed with a sort of fantastical mount: He is seated upon the angels who bear Him. These cherubim's mission is to transport Him in His glory.

In Ezekiel's visions, their appearance is even more amazing in that they are "tetramorphs" ("quadruple shape"), fantastical beings with four pairs of wings and four sides: a human side in front, a lion side on the right, a bull side on the left, and an eagle side in back—all attributes found in the Apocalypse of John (Revelations), as well.

Christian tradition, wishing to see in the New Testament the realization of Old Testament prophecies, interprets Ezekiel's vision of the tetramorph as a symbol of the four evangelists, or the four pillars of divine glory.

⚛ DIVINE MESSENGERS ⚛

Angels were created to sing praise to God, but they also have other missions on earth. They are seen as helpful companions to humans; in the Old Testament, angels comfort and console the afflicted. When the prophet Elijah fled the wrath of Queen Jezebel, a worshipper of Baal who blamed Elijah for undermining her cult, an angel brought him a cake baked on hot stones and a vessel of water, giving him strength to climb the mountain of God and witness a divine apparition.

Angels also protect and intercede for humans, stand by them in daily life, instruct them, and reveal great mysteries.

Some Jewish communities, such as the Essenes (whom we know more about since the discovery of the Dead Sea scrolls), placed great importance on angels and believed that all human activity was constantly under their watchful gaze.

Not surprisingly, Jesus mentions angels in his teachings, citing those in the heavens who protect children and see God in the full brilliance of His light. Although not named as such, these are clearly guardian angels.

Les Anges
pasteurs de nos âmes,
portent nos messages
à Dieu,
et nous rapportent les siens.

(St Jean de la Croix.)

T.F. ÉDIT. PONTIF^{le}   PARIS. PL. 143 bis

Angels, shepherds of our souls, carry our messages to God, and bring His to us in return. —ST. JOHN OF THE CROSS

WHAT DO ANGELS DO?

In the Apocalypse of John (Revelations), certain angels are thurifers, a special term for incense bearers. Incense is the supreme offering to God: its smoke rising to the sky symbolizes prayer rising to the divinity. In this way, the angels transmit the requests and prayers of humanity. One angel's task for all eternity is to present to God the prayers of the saints.

Because angels travel between heaven and earth, they render to God accounts of human actions. In some texts, they report to the archangel Michael. Either way, God goes by their word in treating humans according to their merits.

At the moment of death, a person's soul is carried to the heavens by angels called psychopomps. Many deathbed scenes, written and painted, depict the guardian angel or a host of angels bearing the soul of the deceased, clearing the pathway to heaven, accompanying the soul in the long ascension to protect it from demons, and delivering it to "the breast of Abraham."

THE FALL OF THE
REBELLIOUS ANGELS

At the start of Genesis chapter 6, before the flood—meaning before God's decision to exterminate everything on earth, human and animal, and the episode of Noah's ark—there is mention of creatures called *B'nai Elohim*. Some Bible scholars say these were humans, perhaps descendants of Seth, the third son of Adam and Eve; others say they were divine or semidivine beings: angels.

The enigmatic passage notes the *B'nai Elohim's* attraction to women, with whom they join and procreate. This fornication, forbidden by God, leads to the angels' fall. Hence the expression, "the sin of angels" or "folly of angels." These fallen angels become Satan and his legions of demons, often depicted in texts as lustful and obsessive. Incubi appear and seduce women; succubi conquer men, often intruding at night to take advantage of their erotic dreams.

Although this kind of union between divinities and humans is found in other religions, such as Greco-Roman mythology, in Christianity the transgression is absolutely negative. The origin of evil is identified as the violation of established divine order, which sets a clear boundary between celestial creatures and human beings.

THE HEAVENLY ARMIES

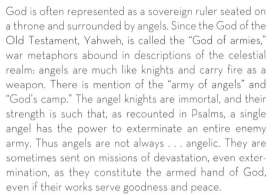

God is often represented as a sovereign ruler seated on a throne and surrounded by angels. Since the God of the Old Testament, Yahweh, is called the "God of armies," war metaphors abound in descriptions of the celestial realm: angels are much like knights and carry fire as a weapon. There is mention of the "army of angels" and "God's camp." The angel knights are immortal, and their strength is such that, as recounted in Psalms, a single angel has the power to exterminate an entire enemy army. Thus angels are not always . . . angelic. They are sometimes sent on missions of devastation, even extermination, as they constitute the armed hand of God, even if their works serve goodness and peace.

In apocalyptic texts, angels of destruction carry out God's wrath and annihilate His enemies. Some theologians consider them actual demons under God's command. The best-known of these texts and the only one found in the New Testament, the Apocalypse of John (Revelations), asserts that seven angels blowing trumpets will announce the Day of Judgment, accompanied by destroyer angels including the Angel of the Abyss, or "exterminating angel," at the head of a devastating army of locusts.

Artists have taken free rein with such violent texts. Renaissance painter Raphael's *St. Michael Vanquishing Satan* depicts Michael, who leads the army in the last days of the world, confronting the dragon, Satan. He strikes the dragon down by armed force, chains it up for a thousand years, and casts it into the abyss.

⚜ THE SONG OF ANGELS ⚜

The primary mission of angels is to ceaselessly sing praise to God. In the Book of Isaiah as well as the Apocalypse of John, it is largely seraphim who sing God's praise, repeating three times: "Holy, holy, holy Lord, His glory fills the earth." This hymn is called the Trisagion.

In the fourth century, both Basil the Great and Cyril of Jerusalem encouraged believers to recite the same words, and in this way join the celestial armies.

Christian theologians find in the triple repetition of the word "holy" an allusion to the mystery of the Trinity, one God in three persons. This prayer is mentioned officially in the Acts of the Council of Chalcedon (451). It is present in Protestant, Byzantine, and Orthodox rites and is recited during the Catholic Mass and in the veneration of the Cross on Good Friday.

In the Book of Enoch, it is the choir of cherubim who praise the Lord. Angels occupy an important place in this Ethiopic Bible text written two centuries after Jesus Christ. As its authenticity has not been proven, it is not integrated into the corpus of canonical texts, although it has been much studied by scholars. It recounts that Enoch, a biblical patriarch and the father of Methuselah, enters the Holy of Holies in the heavenly temple and, approaching the throne of God, hears cherubim singing to His glory.

QUE MA VOIX,
AVEC CELLE DES ANGES,
MONTE VERS VOUS, SEIGNEUR,
POUR VOUS LOUER, POUR
VOUS BÉNIR.

P. de Pontlevoy

1035. BOUASSE JEUNE, PARIS

May my voice, with that of the Angels, rise to Thee, O Lord,
to praise Thee and bless Thee. **—P. DE PONTLEVOY**

GUARDIAN ANGELS

In the Apocrypha, every human being is watched over by two angels, one on each shoulder. One angel accuses, the other defends; God hears the respective "pleas" and decides the sinner's fate. Similarly, in Judaism and Islam, each person is accompanied by an evil angel who tests the will and a good one who preserves purity. The theologian Origen says that the battle between these good and evil angels takes place within the human soul.

Guardian angels watch over our well-being, protect us during sleep, and intercede for us with God during the night. They awaken us in the morning and help us fend off laziness. We see for these protectors a forerunner of sorts in Greco-Roman antiquity: In Plato's *Dialogues*, Socrates often mentions his *daimon* (δαιμον), or guardian genie. Over the centuries, Plato's philosophy, along with that of Aristotle, would inspire many Fathers of the Church, including Saint Bernard (twelfth century), who sees the angel's role as that of intercessor and overseer of the conscience.

During the Middle Ages, increasing individualism elevated the guardian angels' importance. They began to perform multiple roles, protecting their charge, casting out demons, bearing witness before God, and upon death playing the role of psychopomp. According to Saint Thomas, baptism endows the guardian angel with the power to protect and guide the new Christian.

The feast day of guardian angels used to be the same as Saint Michael's day, but since 1608, it has been established as October 2.

Boumard Fils, Paris - France   18444

THE BREAD OF ANGELS

Angels do not eat, but they lend their name to the sweetest, most nourishing food God provides. When Moses left Egypt and crossed the desert, God promised that bread should rain down from the heavens to feed the chosen people, however much they might need. For forty years, His promise was kept. The miraculous bread is called "manna from heaven." In Psalms and in the Book of Wisdom, manna is referred to as "the bread of Angels" or "the bread of the Strong." It tastes like honey, in flavor adapting to the desires of whoever eats it, so that it is always perfectly delicious.

In his teachings, Jesus compares the manna of the Old Testament, which saved the tribe from famine, with the Bread of Life, which gives eternal life. This lends insight into the symbolism of breaking bread at the Last Supper, the body of Christ offered as sacrifice, and the consecrated host consumed at Mass.

Je vous apporte le pain des Anges
qui vous donnera la vie éternelle.

N. 10028   DEPOSÉ

I bring you the bread of Angels, which shall give you eternal life.

⟩ THE ANGELUS ⟨

Jean-François Millet (1814–1875) wrote, "I painted *The Angelus* thinking of my grandmother, who, upon hearing the church bell ringing while we were working in the fields, always made us stop work to say the Angelus for the souls of the departed."

The Angelus is a prayer that recalls the Annunciation made to the Virgin Mary. Its name comes from the prayer's first word in Latin: "*Angelus Domini nuntiavit Mariæ,*" it begins, meaning "The Angel of the Lord brought word unto Mary." At first recited just in the evening, after the sixteenth century it was repeated three times a day, usually at six a.m., noon, and six p.m., to recall the mystery of Christ's incarnation: in the morning it commemorates the Resurrection, at noon the Passion, and in the evening the Annunciation. In between these devotions, the faithful recite the Hail Mary, and at the end say a prayer to God repeating the message of the angel revealing for the first time the coming Incarnation of Christ.

Another element of the Angelus ritual, especially at night, is chiming church bells to announce the top of the hour, using three short rings. After each ring the prayer is recited.

Some attribute the idea for the Angelus to Saint Francis. It occurred to him, it is said, when he traveled to the Orient and was inspired by observing the calls to prayer in Islamic lands. The Angelus has fallen mostly out of use today.

THOMAS AQUINAS, THE "ANGELIC DOCTOR"

Saints often receive sobriquets from their contemporaries or from later believers who admire their works. Such is the case of Thomas Aquinas. His first nickname was not necessarily flattering: the Dominicans used to call him "the mute ox"! A hefty, imposing figure and a man of few words, the Italian monk (1225–1274) devoted himself to scholarly pursuits. Wherever he went—Naples, Rome, Cologne, Paris—he studied Christian doctrine and sought to assimilate into it the philosophy of Aristotle. In honor of his masterwork, *Summa Theologica*, he was designated the patron saint of Catholic universities and schools.

In this treatise, Aquinas accorded an important place to "pure spirits," or angels, and so he was dubbed with the more serious epithet "the Angelic Doctor." The breadth of his reflections on their nature, their relationship to God and to humans, and the fall of certain angels indicates that such matters were a major concern in his theological vision.

Saint Thomas Aquinas was canonized in 1323. His body lies in the Jacobin church in Toulouse.

S. Thomas Aquinas.

SERVANTS OF JESUS
IN THE GOSPELS

In the stories of the Gospels, angels are in service to Jesus. As though to attest to Christ's divine character, angels appear at key moments in his life, making the events even more extraordinary: the Annunciation, the Nativity, the retreat to the desert, the start of the Passion, the Resurrection. They are also at work in the Ascension, and protect the apostles and members of the early Christian communities. Several times, the Angel of the Lord comes to free imprisoned apostles, as in the case of Peter.

The evangelists Mark and Matthew recount that before embarking on his ministry and his mission, Jesus was led into the desert, where he fasted. Here Satan came to tempt him: Satan led Jesus to the top of the Temple and urged him to cast himself into the void, trusting in the Old Testament's words that angels would bear up the Messiah and shield him from all harm. But Jesus was clearheaded. He refused to jump, and rebuked Satan for invoking the name of God in vain. When the Devil, the tempter, withdrew and ceased his harassment, the angels arrived to serve Jesus.

The Gospel of Luke gives another account of the devotion between Jesus and the angels. While Jesus, soon to be betrayed, prays on the Mount of Olives, soldiers arrive to seize him. Peter draws his sword to protect him, but Jesus has him sheathe his weapon: angels exist to serve him, and should he wish it, his Father would send legions of them.

THE SERAPHIM

Like the cherubim, seraphim are descendants of winged Eastern divinities and, half human, half animal, resemble a griffin or sphinx.

Their name signifies "ardent ones," or "those who burn." Seraphim represent God's burning love, but also His wrath and purifying fire, and are often depicted as red or even on fire.

Often seraphim are shown upright, with three pairs of wings—one pair for flying, one pair to hide their nudity, and the last used to shield their faces so that they do not look directly upon the face of God. But they also occasionally take the form of snakes or dragons, or hold a snake in each hand.

While the cherubim bear the divine chariot from underneath, the seraphim hover above it and shelter it with their unfurled wings. Their chief function is to perpetually sing praise to God.

The Bible story in which seraphim play a major role is that of Isaiah, one of the four great biblical prophets (along with Jeremy, Ezekiel, and Daniel). The revelation of his vocation is extraordinary. In a vision, Isaiah is contemplating God on His throne in all His majesty. The seraphim above chant His praise. Their voices shake the portals, a thick smoke spreads over the altar, and Isaiah, horrified, shouts, "Woe is me!" The man who has constantly denounced moral laxity among the people now believes he is like other sinners, his lips sullied by untruth or blasphemy, his person unworthy to behold the Lord. Then one of the seraphim takes a live coal from the altar and touches it to Isaiah's lips, purifying them. "Your iniquity is taken away, your sin is purged," the angel tells him. In this way, Isaiah is anointed a prophet.

SAINT FRANCIS OF ASSISI, THE "SERAPHIC FATHER"

Born in Assisi in 1181 or 1182, Francis was at first known as the saint of the poor and of lepers, a holy man dazzled by Creation, who spoke with animals and spread peace and charity everywhere. He lived in strict asceticism, and championed the restoration of crumbling churches. His last years were spent in prayer and often isolation. He is one of the most popular saints. He founded the Order of the "Lesser Brothers" (later called the Franciscan Order), which was approved by the Lateran Council in 1215 and confirmed in 1223.

In the late summer of 1224, Francis of Assisi withdrew to Mount La Verna to pray and fast at a monastery. On September 14, the feast day of the Holy Cross, he was visited by a seraph, who hovered near him with six wings of fire. Amid the wings he saw a crucified man. Francis spoke these words: "May I feel in my soul and in my body what Thou hast felt in Thine, the suffering of the Passion and the boundless love that inflamed Thee," and thereupon received the stigmata—marks on his body similar to the wounds of crucifixion upon the martyred Christ.

Francis of Assisi died in 1226. He was canonized in 1228 by Pope Gregory IX, who, after Assisi's experience with the fire-winged angel, conferred upon him the title "Seraphic Father."

ANGELS IN THE MIDDLE AGES

In the early centuries A.D., angels were typically represented in art as young people dressed in white. Later,
so they would not be mistaken for winged pagan divinities, they began to be shown in rich court garb. After the
787 Council of Nicea established that angels possessed
a luminescent, perfect corporeal form, artists felt legiti-
mized in these anthropomorphized depictions. The wings
took on greater importance; the number of pairs of wings
indicated the angel's "rank."

Starting in the twelfth century, Saint Anselm of Can-
terbury and Hildegard von Bingen, among others, gave
new impetus to the contemplation of angels. Hildegard,
a German nun in the Benedictine order, described very
thoroughly the angels in her mystical visions: human in
appearance, with perfect faces, intense light, halos, wings,
and eyes of fire. From this point on, the choice of monastic
life meant a commitment to imitate angels, devoting one-
self entirely to praising God and retiring from the material
world. Paintings show angels visiting monks in their cells to
fortify them against temptation.

Angels are present on the portals of churches, fre-
quently in scenes of Judgment Day; a recurrent theme
is that of Saint Michael weighing souls. Sculptors human-
ized angels, putting tears or nuanced expressions on
their faces. In the cathedrals at Rheims and Arras, angels
look upon the devout with enigmatic smiles.

VERA EFFIGIE DELLA BEATA VERGINE
che si venera nella Chiesa delle Grazie
sul Colle di Covignano presso Rimini.

TRUE IMAGE OF THE BLESSED VIRGIN
worshipped at Grace Church on Covignano Hill near Rimini.

Like as a father has compassion on his children, so the Lord has compassion on those who fear him.

For He knoweth our frame; He remembereth that we are dust.

As for man, his days are as grass: as a flower of the field, so he flourisheth.

For the wind passeth over it, and it is gone and the place thereof shall know it no more.

But the mercy of the Lord is from everlasting to everlasting upon them that fear him, and his righteousness unto children's children.

To such as keep His covenant, and to those that remember his commandments to do them.

The Lord hath prepared his throne in the heavens; and his kingdom ruleth over all.

Bless the Lord, ye his angels, that excel in strength, that do his commandments, hearkening unto the voice of his word.

Bless ye the Lord, all ye his hosts; ye ministers of his, that do his pleasure.

Bless the Lord, all his works in all places of his dominion: bless the Lord, O my soul.

« Je suis le Pain de vie,
Je suis le Pain vivant,
qui est descendu du Ciel. »
(St Jean, chap. VI.)

BOUMARD & FILS   N° 5122   ÉDIT^RS PONT^AUX PARIS.

I am the Bread of Life. I am the living Bread, come down from Heaven.
—ST. JOHN, CHAPTER VI

THE SEVEN ARCHANGELS

The archangels are not like other entities in the heavenly hierarchy: they alone are mentioned by name. However, they do not reside at the summit of this hierarchy—on the contrary, they are next to last. They are in contact with humans, however, and this justifies the use of their names.

The count of archangels, according to theologians, is seven: a sacred number. Different persuasions may recognize some names but not others. The three uncontested names are Michael, Raphael, and Gabriel. The Lateran Council of 746 limited the worship of archangels to the three major figures. The fourth archangel, Uriel (or Oriel), is not recognized by the Roman Catholic Church. The names of the remaining three vary somewhat depending on the text: according to Enoch, they are Raguel, Remiel, and Saraqael, but they are most often called Barachiel, Jehudiel, and Sealtiel, as seen on a fresco in a Palermo church, Santa Maria degli Angeli, where their names are inscribed. The chief function of the seven archangels is to combat demons, to contact humans to make major revelations, or come to their aid in a particular case.

In Islam, the archangels bear the throne of Allah.

S. RAFFAELE ARCANGELO

SAINT MICHAEL, THE ARCHANGEL

Michael is the high prince of the celestial court; his name means "he who is like God." In the Bible, specifically the Book of Daniel, he is presented as the greatest of all entities, the patron and protector of Israel, and is one with the Angel of God. In one of the books of Apocrypha, Michael is sent to Abraham to announce his death.

Michael might be called the champion of the forces of good. He heads the heavenly army as the Angel of Peace, to guard the chosen people; as the Prince of Light, he is the polar opposite of the Prince of Darkness. In the Apocalypse of John (Revelations), he leads troops of angels to battle that great dragon and age-old serpent, the Devil. He is victorious, enchains Satan for a thousand years, and casts him into the abyss.

In another side of Michael's nature dwells mercy, along with patience, especially when someone dies. Many Church Fathers call on the angels to evaluate the souls of the deceased so they may account to God for their actions. Saint Michael is often shown weighing souls, a process called "psychostasis." Saints and virgins are exempt from this appraisal; their souls go directly to heaven, accompanied by angels singing. Saint Michael often escorts the souls as they rise.

S. Michele Arcangelo

THE MIRACLES
OF SAINT MICHAEL

Saint Michael is feted several times during the year. Each feast day commemorates one of his miracles.

September 29, the feast of the three archangels, is the date of Saint Michael's apparition on Mount Gargano in Italy in 493. In the town of Sipontum, a rich man named Gargano owned many herds of animals and pastured them on a mount that bore his name. When one of his bulls ran off, Gargano gave chase and shot an arrow at the beast as it stood in the entrance to a cave. The arrow reversed its course, flew back at the shooter, and wounded him. The bishop heard of this occurrence and ordered three days of fasting and public prayer. On the third day Saint Michael appeared to the bishop, declaring that the grotto was under his protection and that a sanctuary dedicated to the angels should be built there. The bishop gave the order at once.

May 8 commemorates the archangel's apparition to Pope Gregory the Great in 590. The plague was devastating Rome at the same time the Lombards were threatening to invade and the Tiber was flooding the city. The pope mounted processions of penitence and had litanies recited. After one of the processions Saint Michael appeared to the faithful; standing atop the Mausoleum of Hadrian, he wiped blood from his sword and returned it to its scabbard. To honor this event, a chapel was built on the peak of the fortress with a statue of the archangel. It was thenceforth know as the Castel Sant'Angelo, or Castle of the Holy Angel.

⚡ MONT SAINT-MICHEL ⚡

The site occupied by Mont St-Michel today was originally a place of worship where Celts and Romans honored Belenus and Jupiter, respectively. But in 709, Saint Michael appeared to Aubert, the pious bishop of Avranches, and asked him to build a sanctuary on the island of Mount Tombe similar to the one on Mount Gargano in Italy. The bishop did so, founding a chapel that became the abbey of Mont Saint-Michel. Pilgrims have traveled to the spot ever since. Saint Michael was chosen as the patron saint of France, and his feast day became the national holiday. Childebert and Charlemagne both went to pray in the sanctuary, as did William the Conqueror, Saint Louis, Philip the Fair, and practically all the kings of France.

Louis XI, especially devoted to the saint, went there to pray three times and in 1469 created the Order of Saint Michael for his chosen knights. He gave each of the thirty-six knights a golden necklace with a medallion bearing an image of the archangel slaying the dragon. After Louis XIV, the order largely consisted of writers, artists, and magistrates. Those knights wore a black cord and an enameled gold cross. The order was dissolved in 1791, then re-created in 1816, and permanently abolished after the July 1830 revolution.

DEVOTION TO SAINT MICHAEL

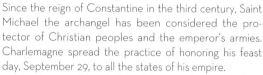

Since the reign of Constantine in the third century, Saint Michael the archangel has been considered the protector of Christian peoples and the emperor's armies. Charlemagne spread the practice of honoring his feast day, September 29, to all the states of his empire.

As the armed hand of God, Saint Michael symbolizes resistance to oppression, and was hence the perfect figure to counsel and accompany Joan of Arc. After the Council of Trent, he took on another aspect, that of the warrior who militarily defends the faith against Protestant heresy. The Order of Saint Michael came about later on; it was the highest order of knighthood in France.

In Islam, he is called Mikail and rules the winds, plant life, and harvest crops.

During World War II, French parachute troops chose Saint Michael as their patron saint. Even earlier, he was the patron saint of bakers, pastry chefs, coopers, and fencers.

SAINT RAPHAEL

The name Raphael means "God healeth," and in the Bible story this archangel is the central figure in the Book of Tobit. In Nineveh, the capital of Assyria, lives the elderly Tobit, who has gone blind. Poor and sick, he sends his son, Tobiah, to retrieve a sum of money held for him in another town. Tobiah hires a man to protect him on his trip. Suddenly, on the banks of the Tigris, a huge fish rises from the water. His servant suggests that Tobiah catch it and keep its heart, liver, and bile to use in ointments. Once at his destination, Tobiah meets Sarah, a young Jew whose seven fiancés have all been killed by the demon Asmodeus. Tobiah decides to wed her and avenge her. He burns the fish's heart and liver; the smoke weakens the demon, who is then captured. Tobiah returns to his father's home with his new bride. Rubbing the fish bile on his father's eyes, he restores his sight. Only then does his companion reveal his true identity: he is the archangel Raphael.

Based on this story, Raphael became the archangel who accompanies and advises travelers. He is also charged with protecting towns and provinces, as well as individual missions, and is the patron saint of travelers by land, sea, and air. Perhaps for this protective function, he has become the patron saint of military intelligence services. In popular faith, he is the patron saint of pharmacists. His feast day, October 24, dates to the twelfth century, and he is celebrated on September 29 along with Michael and Gabriel.

Gabriel's name means "strength of God," or "God is my strength." He is considered the right arm of God and is often depicted as a strapping figure of a man. His feast day is March 24, and he is also celebrated on September 29 along with the archangels Michael and Raphael.

His chief role is to serve as God's messenger, bringing good news. In the Bible, he interprets Daniel's visions and reveals the coming of Christ. Naturally, it is he who announces the birth of Saint John the Baptist and the birth of Jesus.

In Islam, Gabriel is called Djibril and is the most important of all the angels, the one who transmits the divine Revelation to the Prophet. He is sometimes called the Holy Spirit in the Muslim religion.

Because of his messenger function, popular belief has made Gabriel the patron saint of ambassadors, radio and television workers, postal workers, and military communications personnel.

There is little information to be found about the four archangels who, along with the principal three, bring the total to seven. For some sense of them, one can draw details from the Ethiopic Book of Enoch (sometimes spelled Henok or Henoch), a text of contested authenticity.

Uriel (or Oriel). His name means "flame of God" or "light of God." He is the guide of the stars, the keeper of the flames of Hell, and the guardian of light for all the heavenly bodies. He is probably a product of Babylonian influence on the Bible. In fact, in the cuneiform script of Mesopotamia, the sign denoting a god or genie is a star. The Roman Church does not recognize this archangel's name and does not revere him, but he is much in evidence in Eastern Christianity, guarding God the All-Powerful alongside the three main archangels around the Pantocrator (icon of Christ in Majesty).

Barachiel. His name means "blessings of God." He is said to combat idleness, indifference, and wavering faith. He impels believers to be zealous and attentive to God's will. Souls must always be alert and dedicated to religion. His aid is invoked especially for preachers and for propagation of the faith. White roses are hidden in a fold of his mantle.

Jehudiel. His name means "praise of God." He combats envy and jealousy and is called upon in certain exorcisms to drive out a jealous spirit. He encourages kindness, love of one's neighbor, and acceptance of divine decrees. In his right hand is a crown, bestowed in recompense to those who have been faithful to God, and in his left he holds a lash with three thongs to castigate wrongdoers.

Selaphiel (or Sealtiel). His name means "prayer of God." He fights debauchery and drunkenness, and helps believers remain abstinent to combat these vices. He distributes divine grace and offers human repentance to God. He sometimes holds in his right hand a basket of flowers, symbolizing one's delight in God. Otherwise, his hands are clasped in prayer.

⇥ "HERESIES" AND ANGELS ⇥

The historical landscape of the Christian religion is strewn with episodes in which minority communities are rejected for professing a different faith, known as a "heresy." In the twelfth and thirteenth centuries, one of the most influential heresies unfolded against the Cathars, culminating in the Albigensian crusade and Medieval Inquisitions.

Concentrated in the Languedoc region of Southern France, the Cathars believed in two principles of equal strength, good and evil, or God and Satan. God was goodness and light, and created the invisible spiritual world; Satan, lord of evil and darkness, created the visible material world. The human body was therefore created by Satan, and within each body an angel of light was imprisoned. This imprisonment was hell; instead of an afterlife beyond this world, many Cathars believed in reincarnation. As they believed the son of God would never become flesh incarnate, they denied Christ's crucifixion as atonement, believing he was simply an angel.

In reaction, the Fourth Lateran Council (1215) established church doctrine regarding angels and demons: There is a sole and unique creator of all things in existence, visible and invisible, namely God. Angels are among the entities he has created. The human being, including the human body, is the work of God.

SALVIAMO UN'ANIMA!

N. 92

DÉPOSÉ

THE CITY OF ANGELS

One may hear a note of irony when Los Angeles is referred to as the "City of Angels." Yet its inhabitants, called Angelenos, are indeed under the patronage of angels. The city's full name is *Pueblo de Nuestra Señora de Los Ángeles del Río de Porciúncula,* or "Village of Our Lady of the Angels on the Porciúncula River." Why this name?

The locale of the *pueblo* was chosen by the Franciscan friar Juan Crespi on Wednesday, August 2, 1769. In the calendar of his order, this was the feast day of Our Lady of the Angels of Porziuncula, from the name of the church in Italy where Saint Francis of Assisi spent his last days. In 1212, the saint had received a dilapidated chapel situated on "a tiny plot" of Benedictine property. He restored it with his own hands. Later it became a site of worship and a pilgrimage destination. A fresco of the Virgin Mary surrounded by angels was painted above the altar, hence the chapel's name.

It was hard to draw colonists from Mexico to this minuscule settlement. It took twelve years to gather from their ranks eleven men, eleven women, and twenty-two children at Mission San Gabriel (yet another angel name) to inhabit the *pueblo.* They joined the few soldiers, Native Americans, and missionaries present on September 4, 1781. The feast day of Our Lady of Angels was then moved to that date to celebrate the birth of the town.

⚸ AN ANGEL PASSES ⚸

When conversation suddenly ceases and the participants fall quiet and dreamy, one traditional phrase to break the silence is, "An angel passes . . ."

Several origins have been suggested for this expression. One humorous explanation is that the expression came from convents of young girls: only the passage of an angel could create this miraculous little silence amidst their chatter. Another theory supposes that perhaps an abrupt, weighty silence between people inspired them to invoke angels to dispel the tension.

A more academic hypothesis is that the expression comes from a Greco-Roman observance for Mercury-Hermes, the god of commerce and of eloquence. In antiquity, everyone was supposed to be silent in his presence; the expression "Hermes passes" is found in the work of the Greek author Plutarch. And since Hermes has winged heels and serves as messenger of the gods, it makes sense that the phrase was adapted to refer to Christian angels. This saying is common to many languages, including French, Spanish, Hungarian, and German as well as English.

SERIF 1071

THE MASS OF THE ANGELS

Gregorian chant, a form of sacred singing, is inherited from several traditions. The early Christian communities, both Eastern and Western, freely invented their ritual chants. Beginning in the fourth century and through the sixth century, the Roman repertoire differed from the one in Gaul; in the seventh century, the two cultures intersected in Metz, where a famous school for cantors created the *cantilena metensis*, also known as "Metz chant." A century later, this intonation came to be called the "Gregorian chant."

Legend attributes the chant's creation to Pope Gregory the Great, but historians assert it was an encounter between a Frankish king, Pepin the Short, and a pope residing in Gaul under his protection that led to the cultural exchange. In 745, Chrodegang, the bishop of Metz, had the Roman ritual adopted, adjusting it as he did so. Charlemagne, Pepin's son, brought it into his empire. The patronage of Gregory the Great lent this new chant the prestige it enjoys today. The repertoire of Gregorian chant includes the very famous *Mass of the Angels* (*Missa de angelis*), said to go back to the twelfth century. The chant is performed a cappella, without musical accompaniment; that way the singer is freed to absorb the angelic chant in continuous praise of God.

The term "Mass of the Angels" was also traditionally used to refer to the solemn funeral rites held over the coffin upon the death of a child under seven years of age.

NAMING THE ANGELS

While there are thousands of angel names, few of them are widely known. The explanation lies in the successive church councils who established doctrine regarding angels. In 745, the Lateran Council forbade the invocation of angels by name except for veneration of the three angels named in the Holy Scriptures—Michael, Gabriel, and Raphael—considering the rest "of demoniacal essence." In 789, the Council of Aix confirmed the decision and forbade the invention of names for the angels; theologians feared that angels would become pagan idols.

Contested texts such as the Book of Enoch, the Book of Jubilees, and several Apocalypses, along with rabbinical, mystical, or esoteric traditions, give us additional angels' names. Some theories suggest the multiplicity of divinities and spirits in the Sumerian religion brought about the proliferation of angel names by cross germination between the spiritual narratives. In the Bible, however, the emphasis is on the facets of divine will and providence that angels carry out. The ethereal beings are seen almost as allegories of God's attributes, not divinities to be honored unto themselves.

The names we do find for angels correspond to their functions. Most include the suffix -el, meaning God: Oriphiel means "horde of God," Samael, "poison of God"; Phanuel, the angel of repentance who prevents the demons from denouncing people's sins to God, translates as "face of God." Other examples include Anael, "pardon

of God"; Raguel, "friend of God"; Zahariel, "hurricane of God"; and Matariel, "rain of God." The suffix *-yah*, which also means God, from Yahweh, is also common for angel names; the name Suryah, for example, translates as "command of God."

The creation of names plays a sort of magical initiation role in Kabbalistic mysticism. The twenty-two letters of Hebrew correspond with numbers in a complex system, with each angel's name leading to numerical calculations that reveal their characteristics.

A type of occult power comes into play here: by naming, one shares the power of the entity named. In addition to the names that are known and permissible to pronounce, there are others, hidden and secret, that one must never speak. In popular faith and esoteric doctrine, the cult of angels developed around these superstitions. Magical incantation of their names is practiced to repel certain sicknesses thought to originate from demonic influences, as in a ritual of calling upon the archangel Michael to cure migraines. In New Age beliefs, establishing a relationship with one's guardian angel and discovering the angel's name is part of mystical initiation.

THE BIRTH OF
JOHN THE BAPTIST

In the Gospels, several apparitions of angels announce the birth of John the Baptist and the birth of Jesus. These extraordinary events attest to the divine character of the Messiah. As Luke tells us, Zacharias and Elizabeth were a very pious but childless, aging couple. Zacharias was a respected priest. As he ministered in the temple with the faithful waiting outside, an angel appeared to him near the altar. He was seized with fear, but the angel reassured him and announced that his wife was to conceive a child. This child, moreover, would become a prophet, leading masses of people to the Lord. When Zacharias questioned him, the angel introduced himself: it was Gabriel. For failing to believe the archangel's words immediately, Zacharias was struck dumb until the day his son was born.

✨ THE ANNUNCIATION ✨

The angel Gabriel's visit to Mary is called the "Annunciation." He comes to see her and greets her with the first words of the *Ave Maria*, or "Hail, Mary." Calming the awed young woman, Gabriel explains that she will give birth. She is astonished, as she is a virgin, but the archangel assures her that the Holy Ghost is the origin of this extraordinary conception. Mary then submits to her fate: "I am the servant of the Lord," she says.

In Matthew, Gabriel appears to Joseph in his sleep to announce that Mary is carrying a child placed in her womb by the Holy Ghost, and he must not repudiate her. When he awakes, Joseph follows this order to the letter. Later, also in a dream, an angel warns him that he must flee so that Jesus will escape the Massacre of the Holy Innocents. And upon the death of Herod, when the danger has passed, an angel tells him in another dream to return to Egypt.

Annonciation de la Sainte Vierge!

⌁ THE NATIVITY ⌁

Angels are present to rejoice at Jesus's birth, and spread the news of His arrival. Joseph and Mary travel to Bethlehem to fulfill the requirements of the Roman census. Upon their arrival, Mary realizes that it is time to give birth. As there is no room at any of the inns, the couple settle in a manger for animals, where the young woman gives birth to a son during the night. Nearby, shepherds are watching their flocks in the fields when an intense supernatural light suddenly fills the sky, and an angel appears. Although they are afraid at first, he announces to them a joyous event: a savior is born. A multitude of angels joins the first and they all sing the hymn *Gloria in Excelsis Deo*. Then they rise again into the sky and, guided by a star, the shepherds go directly to the manger to give homage to the infant Jesus. This is known as the Adoration of the Shepherds.

THE RESURRECTION OF CHRIST

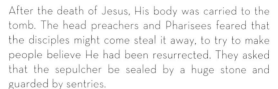

After the death of Jesus, His body was carried to the tomb. The head preachers and Pharisees feared that the disciples might come steal it away, to try to make people believe He had been resurrected. They asked that the sepulcher be sealed by a huge stone and guarded by sentries.

Miraculously, before the terrified, quaking guards, the tomb was opened: Amidst a great clamor and bright light, an angel descended from the heavens and rolled aside the boulder, then knelt as Jesus walked out. Not far away, unaware of the event, a group of devout women who had set out early in the morning to anoint the body were wondering among themselves how they might move the giant stone, when they felt the earth tremble. Upon their arrival, they found the tomb open; they went inside, and found that Jesus had disappeared. But an angel seated on the right side of the tomb explained that Christ had indeed been resurrected. The women returned to tell the disciples. Peter and John, incredulous, returned to the sepulcher, accompanied by the disconsolate Mary Magdalene. The two men entered and found the shroud and linen strips, but did not find the body. Mary Magdalene awaited them outside. Two angels appeared, sitting on the tomb, and asked her why she was weeping. A man arose behind her and asked the same question. At the sound of his voice, she recognized Jesus and fell at his feet. He sent her to bear the news of His resurrection.

ANGELS IN THE JEWISH TRADITION

According to the Talmud, angels came from Babylon with the Israelites, and some of their names are borrowed from Persian religion. They were created on the second day, and their substance is half water and half fire.

Each angel serves a particular capacity. Michael is the guardian of the children of Israel; Gabriel restores strength and courage; Uriel ("light of God") brings light to human beings amidst darkness; and Raphael heals physical and spiritual ills.

During Yom Kippur, according to tradition, every believer must behave like an angel, indulging in neither food nor drink.

Before beginning the Sabbath meal, participants sing the joyful *Shalom Aleichem*, a Jewish liturgical poem. The song welcomes the angels, who make sure the household is well kept and that all is proper for the ceremony and then will report to God: "Peace be upon you, ministering angels, messengers of the Most High, the King of Kings."

Legend has it that on the evening of the Sabbath, every Jew is accompanied by two angels. If the candles are lit, the good angel will bestow a benediction; if they are not lit, it is left to the evil one.

לשנה טובה תכתבו

A happy New Year

אַ װעה: אין דזימעל דאָרט
געהט אױף דײן ד:עלער שטערען;
דו װערסט מיס מזל הײ:יאָר
אַ כלה װערען.

MAIMONIDES AND THE ANGELS

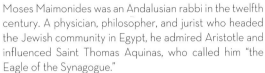

Moses Maimonides was an Andalusian rabbi in the twelfth century. A physician, philosopher, and jurist who headed the Jewish community in Egypt, he admired Aristotle and influenced Saint Thomas Aquinas, who called him "the Eagle of the Synagogue."

Maimonides called angels "intelligences," a word that is also used to refer to powers of the stars. (In another etymological pairing of these heavenly bodies, in Hebrew, the root *Saba* is shared by "Sabaism," meaning "worship of the stars," and "Sabaoth," meaning "angelic armies.") He believed that ancient Jewish tradition acknowledges ten degrees, or orders, of angels, but divided them into two classes: "permanent" angels, who are eternal, and "perishable" angels, who are created at a given point in history. For him the prophets were also angels, sent by God.

Like other theologians, Maimonides asserted that angels are normally invisible but take human form to make themselves accessible to the faint intelligence of humans. He wrote, "Each time there is mention of the vision or word of an angel, it is a prophecy or a dream."

לשנה טובה תכתבו

"THE ASSUMPTION OF THE VIRGIN"

LUIS PONCE DE LEON (1527-1591)

Lady! thine upward flight
The opening heavens receive with joyful song:
  Blest, who thy garments bright
  May seize, amid the throng,
And to the sacred mount float peacefully along.

  Bright angels are around thee,
They that have served thee from thy birth are there:
  Their hands with stars have crowned thee;
  Thou,—peerless Queen of air,
As sandals to thy feet the silver moon dost wear.

  Celestial dove! so meek
And mild and fair!—oh, let thy peaceful eye
  This thorny valley seek,
  Where such sweet blossoms lie,
But where the sons of Eve in pain and sorrow sigh.

  For if the imprisoned soul
Could catch the brightness of that heavenly way,
  'T would own its sweet control
  And gently pass away,
Drawn by its magnet power to an eternal day.

BOUASSE-JEUNE Cie FRANCE

644

THE ANGEL OF FATIMA

Fatima is a small town in Portugal eighty miles north of Lisbon. The village is famed worldwide today for the reported apparitions of the Virgin before three young shepherd children in 1917. Less well known is the fact that an angel had appeared to the children during the previous two years.

Lucia, an eight-year-old shepherd girl, was reciting the rosary in the countryside with two other young girls when, she recounted, a sort of statue made of snow appeared in midair, then disappeared when they finished the rosary. The same thing happened two more times, but when they told their parents of the event, they were scolded for lying. The following year, in the spring of 1916, Lucia was with two cousins close to her age, Francisco and Jacinta, when the angel appeared again, after a vehement gust of wind. This time the angel spoke to them, saying that he was the Angel of Peace, and had them pray with him. In midsummer he again appeared to them. He urged them to engage in prayer and sacrifice, and this time declared himself the Angel of Portugal. Finally, in autumn, while the children prayed in a cave, the same white, luminous, almost transparent figure appeared, holding a chalice in one hand and the Host in the other. The angel spoke in prayer and made himself known as the Angel of the Eucharist. These apparitions, which the children kept to themselves in fear of another scolding, are now considered early signs that the Virgin would appear the following year.

SAINT FRANCES AND
HER GUARDIAN ANGEL

Francesca Bussi de Leoni was born in 1384 to a noble family in Rome. She wished to enter a convent, but her father insisted she marry. She accepted her fate and was a perfect wife and mother to three children. Tragically, her son Evangelista died as a small boy.

One morning at dawn, as she gazed fondly on her sleeping daughter, Evangelista appeared to her in a blinding flash of light, accompanied by an archangel. The boy said that the angel had brought him to stay by her side and console her, because his sister would soon go to heaven as well. His words, alas, came true.

Frances then devoted the rest of her life to charity. After her husband's death, she joined a convent, where she died in 1440. She was canonized in 1608. She is traditionally depicted accompanied by her guardian angel, who continued to protect her throughout epidemics and wars and stand by her during the trials of her life.

S. Francesca.
Ste Françoise. ✤ ✤ S. Francisca
Hl. Francisca. ✤ St. Franzisca.

ANGELS IN PROTESTANTISM

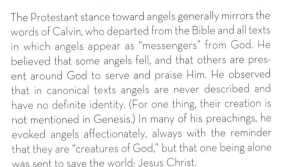

The Protestant stance toward angels generally mirrors the words of Calvin, who departed from the Bible and all texts in which angels appear as "messengers" from God. He believed that some angels fell, and that others are present around God to serve and praise Him. He observed that in canonical texts angels are never described and have no definite identity. (For one thing, their creation is not mentioned in Genesis.) In many of his preachings, he evoked angels affectionately, always with the reminder that they are "creatures of God," but that one being alone was sent to save the world: Jesus Christ.

Calvin broke away from the Roman Catholic Church of his day, which had developed rituals and feast days in honor of angels. In his view, one must never venerate angels, worship them, or ask them to intercede with God in one's favor. He believed his doctrine was in accordance with that of Saint Paul.

FRA ANGELICO, "PAINTER OF ANGELS"

The man known as "the painter of angels" had several actual names: at birth he was called Guidolino Di Pietro; as a monk, Fra Giovanni da Fiesole; and finally he became Fra (or Beato) Angelico. He lived in Italy in the fifteenth century, during a rich period of artistic and cultural activity called the *quattrocento*. His art bridged medieval values and the revitalization that inspired the first Renaissance. After his art studies in Florence, he entered a Dominican order and became a priest in 1427, when his fame as an artist was rapidly spreading. He created works for the San Domenico da Fiesole church, the Convent San Marco in Florence (on commission from the Medicis), and the main chapel at Saint Peter's in Rome. Fra Angelico dedicated himself to painting religious subjects, votive art, altarpieces, and frescoes. He became the model for a school of miniaturists and painters in Florence, and his treatment of light would have a strong influence on the later course of Italian painting.

THE TARES AND
THE HEAVENLY HARVEST

In the Epistles of Paul, angels or archangels are the heralds announcing the end of the world. They render homage to the Lord as he descends to preside over the last judgment.

In the Gospels of Matthew and Mark, angels not only witness the judgment but thereafter carry out the punishments that are ordained, fulfilling the parable of the good seed and the tares, or the "heavenly harvest."

In this parable, Jesus tells how tare, an evil weed, has been sown by demons in a wheat field. Rather than try to separate the seeds in the field, He says, let them all grow. Harvest time is the moment to separate the plants, when it will be clear which are the bad weeds to gather and burn, while keeping aside the wheat.

Jesus then delivers the key to the parable with the declaration that the angels shall be the reapers for the heavenly harvest on Judgment Day: They will separate the evildoers from the just and cast the wicked into the flames. Before the final cataclysm, when the sun and moon disappear and the stars fall from the sky, the Savior will send angels who, with the sound of their trumpets, will gather the chosen ones.

SHEPHERDS AND ANGELS

Ever since the announcement of the Nativity by angels to shepherds, there has been a certain historical complicity between the two. Several legends recount similar events.

Felix Porri was a twelve-year-old shepherd boy in Cantalice, Italy, who left his flock in the care of Providence to attend church services. He was replaced in the fields by his guardian angel—witnesses declared they had seen him at work! Later on, at age twenty-eight, the shepherd became a Capuchin friar in Rome, Fra Felix. He died in ecstasy in 1587, at age seventy-two, before the Virgin and all the angels.

During the same time period, nearly the same thing happened to young Jorge de Calzado in Spain. Jealous fellow shepherds denounced him to their master, who decided to keep watch on the boy. Seeing the guardian angel appear, he was dumbfounded. Jorge explained to him that the angel takes over while he goes to Mass, and the master decided to keep him on. Jorge entered a Franciscan order at age thirty. He became a spiritual master, enlightened by his guardian angel.

Pascual Baylon (1540–1592), another Spanish shepherd who became a Franciscan, did not abandon his flock to attend Mass, but dwelt upon it in his mind so deeply that his guardian angel appeared to proffer him the Host and let him worship the Holy Sacrament. Legend says that the angels taught him to read and write. He was canonized in 1691.

M on Ange,
marchera devant vous
et vous gardera en chemin.
(Exode.)

BOUASSE-LEBEL 2412 PARIS.

My Angel will go before you and will keep you on the way.

"GUARDIAN ANGEL FROM HEAVEN SO BRIGHT"

TRADITIONAL HYMNAL, AUTHOR UNKNOWN

Guardian angel from heav'n so bright,
Watching beside me, to lead me aright,
Fold thy wings around me, O guard me with love,
Softly sing songs to me, of heav'n above.

Beautiful angel, my guardian mild,
Tenderly guide me, for I am thy child.

Angel so holy! whom God sends to me,
Sinful and lowly, my guardian to be,
Wilt thou not cherish the child of thy care?
Let me not perish, my trust is thy prayer.

Beautiful angel, my guardian mild,
Tenderly guide me for I am thy child.

O may I never forget thou art near:
But keep me ever in love and fear.
Waking and sleeping, in labor and rest,
In thou sweet keeping my life shall be blest.

Beautiful angel, my guardian mild,
Tenderly guide me for I am thy child.

Angel, dear Angel oh, close by me stay;
Safe from harm shield me, all ill keep away—
Then thou wilt lead me when this life is o'er
To Jesus and Mary to praise evermore.

Beautiful angel, my guardian mild,
Tenderly guide me for I am thy child.

SOUVENEZ-VOUS, Ô, MON BON ANGE-GARDIEN, QUE LE
SEIGNEUR VOUS AYANT CONFIÉ LE SOIN DE MON
ÂME, VOUS EN ÊTES DEVENU LE PROTECTEUR ET
L'AMI. PROTÉGEZ-MOI, DIRIGEZ-MOI.

E. M. Br.   MADE IN BELGIUM   O-2

*Remember, O kind Guardian Angel, that the Lord has entrusted to you the
care of my soul, you are its protector and friend. Protect me and guide me.*

WHY WE SPEAK OF "HOLY ANGELS"

While "holiness" can describe a person notable for unstinting obedience to divine decrees, proximity to God, an elevated mind, and exemplary influence on others, angels have a particular status regarding the holy state. Pure, immaterial spirits, they were created to sing God's praise and to serve Him. Some among them rebelled, and others remained faithful. The catechism tells us that the faithful ones remain forever in a state of perfect holiness and joy, which they shall never lose for all eternity.

Some scholars say that before the original sin, human beings were created to be the tenth order of angels—the lowest—but after the fall, were cast out by God, who installed heavenly guardians to the east of Eden to prevent the humans' return, expelling them wholly from the heavenly hierarchy. But because of the sacrifice of Christ and the Redemption, the good shall be placed closest to God when they resurrect, above even the highest class of angels, the seraphim.

*Holy Angels, may we approach the Holy Table with the respect and
love you render to God hidden in the Eucharist.*

⇒ "THE HYMN," XI–XIII ⇐

JOHN MILTON (1608–1674)

XI

At last surrounds their sight
A globe of circular light,
That with long beams the shamefaced night arrayed;
The helmèd cherubim
And sworded seraphim
Are seen in glittering ranks with wings displayed,
Harping in loud and solemn choir,
With unexpressive notes to heaven's new-born heir.

XII

Such music (as 'tis said)
Before was never made,
But when of old the sons of morning sung,
While the creator great
His constellations set,
And the well-balanced world on hinges hung,
And cast the dark foundations deep,
And bid the weltering waves their oozy channel keep.

XIII

Ring out, ye crystal spheres,
Once bless our human ears,
(If ye have power to touch our senses so)
And let your silver chime
Move in melodious time;
And let the bass of heaven's deep organ blow;
And with your ninefold harmony
Make up full consort to the angelic symphony.

THE ECSTASY OF
SAINT TERESA OF AVILA

Saint Teresa of Avila was born in 1515. The Spanish saint, canonized in 1622, was a nun who reformed the Carmelite order to which she belonged. In her writings, she recounted many mystical experiences. One day, after she had spent a long time in prayer and was singing a hymn, she entered into a rapture so intense it almost frightened her. A voice told her, "I do not wish you to converse with people anymore, but only with the angels."

A cherub appeared to her several times at her left side: a small creature, very beautiful, with an exalted face, carrying a flaming spear. From time to time, the angel plunged his weapon into the heart of the ecstatic saint. She described a mystical state of extreme pain, yet at the same time an exquisite happiness. This ecstasy arising from the sensation of a pierced heart, like Jesus on the Cross pierced by the Roman soldier's lance, is called "transverberation." Saint Teresa's ecstasy is immortalized in a work by the Baroque sculptor Bernini, created in 1652 for the Cornaro family chapel in Rome's Santa Maria della Vittoria church.

SANTA TERESA DI GESÙ

THE ASSUMPTION OF THE VIRGIN

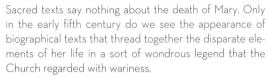

Sacred texts say nothing about the death of Mary. Only in the early fifth century do we see the appearance of biographical texts that thread together the disparate elements of her life in a sort of wondrous legend that the Church regarded with wariness.

It is said that Mary encountered an angel on the Mount of Olives who extended to her a palm from the Tree of Life and announced that her end would come soon. Miraculously, all the apostles returned to gather about her. Jesus appeared, surrounded by angels, and confided his mother's soul to the archangel Michael. This event is called "the Dormition of the Virgin" by many churches, from the Latin word for "sleep," evoking the idea that for saints death is a sort of temporary sleep. Mary was buried, and a few days later Jesus returned to take up her body and carry it to Heaven; this is the Assumption itself. Some in the Roman Catholic Church believe the Assumption includes the journey of both Mary's body and soul.

The feast of the Assumption, established by the Byzantine emperor Maurice in the sixth century, falls on the same date in various calendars, August 15. Before it became officially sanctioned, the feast was a great popular celebration. Catholic dogma regarding Mary was established quite later: 1854 for the Immaculate Conception and 1950 for the Assumption. Protestantism does not include such doctrine.

IMMACULATA

MARY, QUEEN OF ANGELS

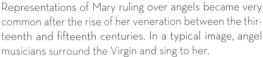

Representations of Mary ruling over angels became very common after the rise of her veneration between the thirteenth and fifteenth centuries. In a typical image, angel musicians surround the Virgin and sing to her.

All the important episodes of Mary's life are marked by apparitions of angels, including the Annunciation by the archangel Gabriel, the Nativity, and the Assumption, in which she is borne up to heaven by angels. And the depiction of angelic music in turn evokes paradise: angels are singing everywhere, sometimes with phylacteries—banners inscribed with the words of chants—floating above their heads. Musician angels are seen in illuminations, chapel frescoes, and church windows.

In the Saint Julien cathedral of Le Mans, a fresco on the ceiling of the Virgin's chapel boasts no fewer than forty-seven angels, fifteen of them playing musical instruments. Interestingly, among the numerous instruments shown is the *vielle*, or fiddle, a profane instrument more often associated with troubadours singing to a lady, here incorporated into the worship of Mary.

Gratitud Nacional - Santiago

THE ANGELS OF
EASTERN CHRISTIANITY

Eastern Christianity often calls the Mass "the Holy Synaxis," meaning the sacred convocation of the people of God, adopting the word that in Orthodox ritual denotes the assembly of saints or angels. Like all God's creatures, human beings are called upon to render glory to God and join the ceaseless praise-giving of the heavenly beings.

Similarly, in the Orthodox calendar, November 8 is celebrated as "the Synaxis of the Chiefs of the Heavenly Hosts, Michael and Gabriel, and the Other Heavenly Bodiless Powers," commemorating Saint Michael's role in reuniting the choirs of angels after the rebellion of Lucifer and the fallen angels.

In Byzantine art, "the Synaxis of the Archangels" is the subject of many works, especially icons, which depict Raphael in priest's garb, flanked by warrior Michael and peaceful Gabriel, all three holding an image of Christ. They symbolize society's religious, military, and civil powers.

Saints Anges de Dieu

qui le voyez face à face
rendez mille actions de grâces
pour moi.

Anc. Manuscrit.

Holy Angels of God, who see Him face to face, render unto
Him a thousand thanks for me.

ANGEL RESCUERS OF MARTYRS

Angels are always on hand to save martyrs of the faith. This was the case for Daniel and his friends.

During the exile in Babylon, a young Jew named Daniel came to the attention of King Darius and became very influential under his reign. Jealous courtiers conspired to issue a decree forbidding anyone to pray to a god other than the one worshipped by the king, on penalty of being thrown to the lions. Daniel, they knew, prayed to Yahweh, the Hebrew God of the Bible, three times a day. He did not cease his pious practice, and the plotters denounced him. Darius, heavy of heart, pronounced the sentence, and Daniel was thrown into the pit of beasts. In the wee hours of the morning, tormented by conscience, Darius went to see what had become of him. Miraculously, Daniel was unharmed. He said to Darius, "My God sent an angel and closed the lions' jaws. They did not hurt me, for I was innocent in His eyes." Darius had him brought out, restored him to his position at court, and had the courtiers cast into the same pit. They were instantly devoured.

A similar fate befell Daniel's companions, Ananias, Azarias, and Misael, known as the "three holy youths of Babylon." Because they refused to bow down to the golden statue the king had erected, they were bound together and thrown into a furnace. However, the three emerged from the fire safe and sound. The king glimpsed the Angel of the Lord amidst the flames and acknowledged the power of their God.

SAINTS ANGES

DE DIEU

QUI LE VOYEZ FACE

À FACE, RENDEZ

MILLE ACTIONS DE

GRÂCES POUR MOI.

Anc. Manuscrit

1032. BOUASSE JEUNE, PARIS

Holy Angels of God, who see Him face to face, render unto
Him a thousand thanks for me.

✄ JOAN'S VOICES ✄

Upon hearing miraculous voices, a little shepherd girl from the village Domrémy rose to become Joan of Arc, the French saint and heroine. Among the voices was that of the archangel Michael, chief of the heavenly hosts, vanquisher of the satanic dragon. During Joan's lifetime, devotion to Michael was particularly fervent; countless pilgrimages were made to Mont St-Michel and Puy-en-Velay. Charles VII had the archangel's image emblazoned on his standards.

At age thirteen, the young girl was alone in a field when she was dazzled by a sudden intense light, and a most noble voice rang out. She understood that it was Saint Michael surrounded by angels. For four years, she received his instruction. And throughout her mission she would be sustained by the voices that spoke to her. In May 1428, during the siege of Orléans, when it was feared that the enemy might overrun Joan's weakened troops, she suddenly doffed her helmet, seeming to salute invisible visitors. She then inspired the courage and confidence of the men fighting with her, telling them that the "companies of her partisans" included troops of angels.

La Vénérable Jeanne d'Arc.

ANGELS OF THE APOCALYPSE

In the Greek language, the word "apocalypse" is synonymous with "revelation," in all its meanings. But over time, since apocalyptic works largely deal with revelations about the end of the world, the word has taken on this particular association. In the Apocalypse, the guides of virtuous souls are often represented as the angels Phanuel ("face of God"), Remiel, Jehiel, or Oriel (also called Uriel).

In the Gospels, Jesus, evoking the end of the world, refers to angels surrounding the Father in His glory. But it is the Son who will mete out justice, to the acclamation of choirs of "myriad upon myriad, thousands upon thousands" of angels. This second coming of the Messiah on earth, awaited by Christians, in theological parlance is called "parousia," meaning "presence." The glorious presence of Jesus rules the world in its entirety at the time of the Apocalypse, and angels bear witness.

THE APOCALYPSE OF JOHN

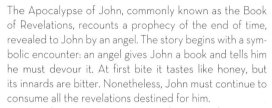

The Apocalypse of John, commonly known as the Book of Revelations, recounts a prophecy of the end of time, revealed to John by an angel. The story begins with a symbolic encounter: an angel gives John a book and tells him he must devour it. At first bite it tastes like honey, but its innards are bitter. Nonetheless, John must continue to consume all the revelations destined for him.

Angels are omnipresent at the Apocalypse. We see them at work guarding the Seven Churches of Asia Minor. As for the "seven angels with seven bowls of the final scourges" (the seven plagues), they point toward the heavenly Jerusalem. It is angels who proclaim the divine decree, carry it out, and confirm the predictions of Christ in his role as final judge. Some bear incense; one eternally transmits the prayers of the saints to God; others hold weapons and engage in the great battle waged by the archangel Michael against the demonic dragon, whom he casts into the abyss.

Finally, in the struggle between the Beast, who represents Satan, and the divine Word, Jesus, angels form a heavenly retinue, dressed in pure white linen and mounted on white horses.

THE TRUMPETS OF JUDGMENT DAY

In the Apocalypse of John (Revelations), it is prophesied that seven angels will blow seven trumpets to signal the catastrophes. At the sound of the first trumpet, hail, fire, and blood will rain down from the heavens; at the second, a burning mountain will plunge into the ocean, killing countless sea animals; at the third, a star falls into the rivers and turns their waters bitter and poisonous. At the sound of the fourth trumpet the sun, moon, and stars grow dim, nearly dark. With the progression, the cataclysm intensifies. The fifth trumpet precipitates the fall of a personified star, which is given the key to the well of the Abyss. The star unlocks the bottomless pit and multitudes of locusts stream out to torture sinners on orders of the Angel of the Abyss (named Abaddon in Hebrew and Apollyon in Greek). The sixth trumpet sounds the call to loose the four angels of the Apocalypse from their chains; these armed horsemen will attack and kill the people of earth. Finally, the sixth and last trumpet announces the adoration of Christ by eighty elders who leave their thrones to bow down to Him while the Heavenly Temple opens its doors to reveal the Ark of the Covenant.

ISIDORE AND THE ANGEL FARMERS

Isidore and his wife lived in Spain. By the grace of Providence, their young son was saved from drowning after he fell into a well, when the water miraculously surged to the top and placed him on its rim. After this, the couple decided to separate and devote their lives to prayer.

But Isidore was a farmer, and the requirements of the pious life posed a problem: How could he reconcile the demands of his work with frequent prayer, especially since he had promised to attend Mass every day? A solution came from the heavens: When it was time for the service each day, Isidore had to leave his field, but God sent angels to perform the work in his stead. Sometimes they pulled the plough in his absence; on different occasions, a second plough pulled by two shining white oxen worked side by side with him. The other farmers, jealous, denounced him to their master, but the master looked kindly upon Isidore, who later brought the master's daughter back to life after she had died.

Isidore worked several other miracles, once causing a fountain of water to spring from dry ground. Today he is the patron saint of Madrid, where he died in 1170. Forty years after his death, when his remains were to be moved, his body was found to be intact. He was canonized in 1622.

ST ISIDORE.

Lorsque nos mains ont touché
des aromates, elles embaument
tout ce qu'elles touchent:
faisons passer nos prières par
les mains de la Ste Vierge,
elle les embaumera.

(Extr. de la Vie du Curé d'Ars.)

Déposé.

When our hands have touched balm, they perfume all they touch: let our
prayers pass through the hands of the Blessed Virgin, she will perfume them.

"EASTER WINGS"

GEORGE HERBERT (1593–1633)

Lord, Who createdst man in wealth and store,
Though foolishly he lost the same,
Decaying more and more,
Till he became
Most poore:

With Thee
O let me rise,
As larks, harmoniously,
And sing this day Thy victories:
Then shall the fall further the flight in me.

My tender age in sorrow did beginne;
And still with sicknesses and shame
Thou didst so punish sinne,
That I became
Most thinne.

With Thee
Let me combine,
And feel this day Thy victorie;
For, if I imp my wing on Thine,
Affliction shall advance the flight in me.

JACOB AND THE ANGELS

One Bible figure who often saw angels is Jacob, the grandson of Abraham. His parents, Isaac and Rebecca, had twin sons, Jacob and Esau. The father's favorite was Esau. Disguising himself as his brother, Jacob obtained a blessing from his blind father. The enmity between the brothers then caused Jacob to flee; he walked until nightfall, then fell asleep, exhausted. As he slept he had an astonishing dream: "There was a ladder set up on the earth, and the top of it reached to heaven; and behold, the angels of God were ascending and descending on it." At the top of the ladder, God in all His light announced that all the land around Jacob would belong to his numerous descendants, that his people would follow him wherever he went, and that he would lead them to the Promised Land.

Jacob stayed away from his father's land for many years. He settled in Mesopotamia, where he raised a family. At last he decided to return to Canaan, the land of Abraham, and face his brother's wrath. When he set out, he sent his family ahead of him, with servants and flocks as gifts to soften Esau's heart. As he traveled on alone, he was suddenly attacked by a mysterious man, with whom he wrestled until dawn. The man then blessed him and told him to take the name "Israel," which means "he who hath struggled with the divine." Jacob realized that the mysterious figure was the Angel of the Lord. Jacob was left with a lame hip, but he had not been vanquished.

SAINT DOMINIC AND THE ANGELS

Saint Dominic lived in Rome at the priory of Saint Sixtus, with his disciples. One day, two of the disciples set off to beg for food for the monks. They were having no success, until at last a woman gave them a loaf of bread. But on their way back to the priory, a man asked them for alms, and so they gave him the bread and returned empty-handed. Dominic welcomed them, saying that the poor man they had encountered was an angel, and they should not worry. He gave the order to call everyone to the refectory for the meal, even though there was nothing to eat or drink. The tables were set and the monks took their places. Suddenly, after the blessing, as a monk read the Bible aloud, two young men appeared with magnificent loaves of bread, which they placed on the table; the men then disappeared. Dominic sent for wine to be brought from the cellar. In a second miracle, the wine cask was full. The company ate and drank for three days and gave the rest to the poor. In his sermon, Dominic spoke of divine Providence, assuring that it provides for those who believe.

VRAI PORTRAIT DE
St DOMINIQUE
conservé à Bologne dans la basilique
du Saint.

True portrait of St. Dominic, preserved in Bologna at the Saint's basilica.

ANGELS, GENIES, AND DEMONS OF ISLAM

Angels hold an important place in Islamic theology. Of the Five Pillars of Islam, the pillar of Faith requires Muslims to believe in angels. Allah is said to have created angels out of Light. They are innumerable and fill space completely. As the celebrated ninth-century imam, At-Tirmidhi, described, "There is no space the width of four fingers, but there is an angel there, bowing his forehead to earth in prostration to God."

In Islam, angels cannot fall into sinfulness. They are asexual and superior to humans and to prophets, except for Muhammad. The angels are of the same nature as genies (or *djinns*) and demons. As in Judeo-Christian tradition, they pray to God, for Muslims Allah, and hold up His throne in the seven heavens.

The angels of the Koran are winged, and never appear as women. They display a variety of other traits and talents, such as slipping beneath the eyelids of other beings to observe the workings of God. They can also infiltrate one's heart. They love light, prayers, and sweet perfumes—these are their nourishment.

In battle, pious Muslims are aided by armies of angels. The angel Djibril (Gabriel), Muhammad says, is endowed with one hundred and forty pairs of wings. It is told that the angel appeared to him one day, placed himself at Muhammad's service, and asked him what his orders might be. And instead of asking the angel to crush his enemies between two mountains, as Djibril himself suggested, the Prophet asked that their descendants worship God.

Muhammad described the angels who bear the immense heavenly throne, declaring that the distance between their shoulder and earlobe equals the distance a fast bird flies in seven hundred years.

The Islamic equivalent of Satan is Iblis (or Eblis); he is not a fallen angel, but a prideful *djinn* who defied God by refusing to bow down to Adam in greeting. There are *djinns* who obey the divine order and are believers, while others are evildoers, called *shayatin*, who become demons.

MUHAMMAD AND THE ANGELS

Traditional lore features several miraculous occasions when angels intervened in the life of the Prophet Muhammad.

First, when Muhammad is six years old, angels seek him out, open his chest, take out his heart, cleanse it of all stain, and fill it with faith and courage before placing it back in his body.

Around 610, as he is meditating in a cave on Mount Hira, Muhammad is visited by the angel Djibril (Gabriel), who reveals himself as the Messenger of God and orders him to spread the divine word. Djibril guides him again when Muhammad flies to the seven heavens on his winged mare, Buraq, to meet Adam, Jesus, John the Baptist, Enoch, Aaron, Moses, and Abraham on the nocturnal voyage recorded in the *hadiths*, or Islamic holy traditions.

It is also told that when the Prophet died, his companions were so absorbed with designating his successor that they forgot to carry out his funeral rites. Hence the angels Djibril and Azrael cared for him in his agony and performed the mortuary offices upon his body.

THE PRINCIPAL ANGELS OF ISLAM

Djibril (Gabriel) is called "the trustworthy spirit." He transmits the Revelation to the prophets. He wears a turban of light. He also gives the Kaaba (Sacred House of God) to Adam and has it rebuilt by Abraham and Ishmael.

Israfil (Raphael) sounds the trumpet of truth on Judgment Day. At the trumpet's first blast, everything on earth is devastated; the second blast signals its resurrection.

Mikail (Michael) was sent by God to bring clay so that He might fashion the first Adam. The earth refused and the angel returned empty-handed. God then sent Azrael, the Angel of Death, and the earth bowed to his will. One day Muhammad asked Djibril, "Why is it that I have never seen Mikail laugh?" Djibril replied, "He laughs no more, now that Hell has been created."

Harut and Marut are two tempter angels who goad humans to commit sin, but warn their victims, saying, "We come to test you." It is up to the individual whether or not to heed.

Azrael is the Angel of Death. It is he who carries off the souls of people who die.

Maalik is the overseer of Hell; **Ridwan** oversees Paradise.

Muslims have the equivalent of guardian angels. Each person is accompanied by two angels, one for good actions, the other for bad ones. They record all one's words and actions. If a sin is committed, the angel waits six hours before putting it in writing, to allow the sinner to repent and beg forgiveness.

In the mosque in Mecca is the Station of Abraham, which enshrines the black stone that the archangel Djibril presented to Abraham as he was rebuilding the Kaaba with his son, Ishmael. In the seventh heaven, directly above the Kaaba, the central place of worship for Muslims, seventy thousand angels are constantly praying.

In Islamic doctrine, 2,000 years before the creation of Adam, the angels gathered in Jerusalem at the place that is now the site of the Mosque of Omar. Also known as the Dome of the Rock, the mosque was built in the seventh century by Sultan Abd al-Malik, high up on a plateau called the Esplanade of Mosques. The shrine sits at the summit of Mount Moriah, above a sacred stone about thirty feet in diameter called the Shetiya (the Rock), revered as the foundation of the world. Jewish tradition places both Abraham's sacrifice of Isaac and Solomon's temple here, while the Muslims believe it is the place from which Muhammad, escorted by Djibril, made his ascension to Paradise.

✣ ANGELS AND SAINT PAUL ✣

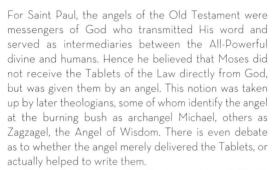

For Saint Paul, the angels of the Old Testament were messengers of God who transmitted His word and served as intermediaries between the All-Powerful divine and humans. Hence he believed that Moses did not receive the Tablets of the Law directly from God, but was given them by an angel. This notion was taken up by later theologians, some of whom identify the angel at the burning bush as archangel Michael, others as Zagzagel, the Angel of Wisdom. There is even debate as to whether the angel merely delivered the Tablets, or actually helped to write them.

But in Paul's view, after the incarnation of Christ, there was no need for angels to be messengers of the Lord: Jesus is the Son of God, and He alone reveals the law. And on Judgment Day, although angels or arch-angels will be heralds announcing the event, it is the Lord who will descend from Heaven to proclaim the end of the world.

Nonetheless, for Paul, angels surround and protect humans on earth, and also guard the celestial Jerusalem, singing praises to God in Paradise, where the just shall go.

Sanctus Paulus, Doctor gentium.

"GREAT SPIRITS NOW ON EARTH ARE SOJOURNING"

JOHN KEATS (1795–1821)

Great spirits now on earth are sojourning—
  He of the cloud, the cataract, the lake,
  Who on Helvellyn's summit, wide awake,
Catches his freshness from Archangel's wing;
He of the rose, the violet, the spring,
  The social smile, the chain for freedom's sake;
  And lo!—whose steadfastness would never take
A meaner sound than Raphael's whispering.
And other spirits there are, standing apart
  Upon the forehead of the age to come.
These, these will give the world another heart
  And other pulses. Hear ye not the hum
Of mighty workings?—
  Listen awhile ye nations, and be dumb!

ELIJAH IN THE DESERT

In many contexts, the word "angel" is synonymous with deliverer of aid and consolation. In the time of Elijah (mid 800s B.C.), Ahab ruled in Israel, and his wife, Jezebel, practiced the illicit worship of Baal and Astarte, false gods, instead of the True God, Yahweh. One day, as a great drought was ravaging the land, God ordered Elijah to summon the prophets of Baal and Astarte to Mount Carmel, and to butcher and prepare two bulls for sacrifice. The pieces of each bull were laid atop a woodpile on two separate altars. Elijah, alone before hundreds of priests, prophets, and people of Israel, challenged the priests to burn their bull in sacrifice. The priests tried and failed. Elijah then poured jars of water on the other bull and invoked the God of Abraham, Isaac, and Jacob. At once, fire rained from the sky and consumed the water. All present fell prostrate upon the ground. Elijah ordered all the priests of Baal be put to death. He prayed earnestly for rain to fall again, and it indeed began. The drought was ended.

Hearing of the events, Jezebel was furious and ordered that Elijah be killed. He fled toward the kingdom of Judah, but the march through the desert so wearied him that he lay down beneath a bush and called death to take him. An angel awoke him, and administered to him with food and water. Elijah slept again, and again the angel wakened him, delivering more sustenance, as the road would be long. This aid was critical, allowing Elijah to continue his march to Mount Sinai, where God appeared to him and presented him with the Tablets of the Law.

S. Elia, Profeta

SAINT PETER DELIVERED
BY THE ANGEL

As recounted in the Acts of the Apostles, King Herod Agrippa I, who ruled Israel under Roman control from A.D. 37 to 44, persecuted the members of the newly emergent Church. He ordered the killing of James, the brother of John, and had Saint Peter imprisoned.

In his cell, bound by two chains and flanked by two soldiers, Peter fell asleep. Sentinels were posted outside. Suddenly, a great light was seen and the Angel of the Lord appeared, tapped Peter on the side, and wakened him, saying to him, "Arise, and make haste!" His chains miraculously fell away, and the Angel told Peter to garb himself and follow him. Peter wondered whether he was dreaming, but he obeyed. They passed two guard posts and found themselves before the iron gate of the city. There, too, the door opened of itself. They walked down a street and the Angel disappeared. Peter realized that he was not dreaming, and that the Angel had indeed delivered him. He went to join his companions.

Herod, in a rage, had the guards killed. Shortly thereafter the king, attired in his royal finery and swelling with pride, was addressing the people when the Angel of God brutally struck him down, for "he gave not God the glory." The holy book says, "Eaten by worms, he died."

Thou art Peter, and upon this rock I shall build my Church, and the gates of Hell shall not prevail against it.

ANGELICA,
OR "THE HERB OF THE ANGELS"

According to legend, it was the archangel Raphael who revealed the properties of a plant from the *Apiaceae* family called angelica, a large *umbellifera* that can reach a height of six feet. In the Middle Ages it occupied an important place in herb gardens. During the Renaissance, it was also called "archangelica," "angels' herb," and "herb of the Holy Spirit." It was considered an effective remedy for scorpion stings, snakebite, and rabies. Elixirs made from the plant were said to guarantee longevity. It was hung around children's necks to protect them from evil charms, as its scent was believed to repel sorcerers.

The Swiss alchemist, astrologer, and physician Paracelsus relates that in Milan, during the plague of 1510, a mixture of wine and powdered angelica would protect one from the disease. (History does not record whether it actually worked.)

All parts of the plant have a use. The leaves add flavor to soups and salads, the root has medicinal properties, and the stalks are candied as treats, especially in the Niort and Marais Poitevin regions of France, where angelica jams and liqueurs are also produced. The monks of Niort developed its use as candy. Its commerce flourished during the eighteenth century, and today it remains a classic ingredient of fruitcake.

Voici Celui qu'adorent les anges. En approchant de Lui avec respect, avec humilité, Il fera en nous des prodiges d'amour.

Bse Angèle de Foligno.

MAISON BOUASSE-LEBEL—Dauverné & Cie   6165   PARIS

Behold Him whom the angels adore. Treating Him with respect, with humility, He will work wonders of love within us.

THE ANGELS OF SODOM

Abraham and his nephew, Lot, set off for the Promised Land, Genesis tells us. But Lot settled in Sodom, on the plain of Jordan. The city of Sodom was a place of evil, its inhabitants without morals, and thus God decided to destroy the city.

To spare Lot and his family, He sent two angels to warn them and enjoin them to leave. When the angels, in the guise of two comely youths, arrived at the portal to the city, Lot spontaneously offered them hospitality, not knowing their identity. That night, ill-intentioned neighbors tried to force their way into Lot's home to seize the two handsome visitors. The angels responded by striking them blind, and blocked the door so that the household could gather and prepare to flee. They told everyone to depart from the city without turning back. Lot's sons-in-law refused, so Lot set off accompanied only by his wife and two daughters. On the road, his wife disobeyed the angels' orders and turned around for a last look back at the city in flames. She was turned into a statue of salt, and Lot and his daughters had to continue on their route to the mountains without her.

Do this in memory of me.

⚛ ANGELS IN MORMONISM ⚛

Joseph Smith, Jr. (1805-1844) was the founder of Mormonism. That religion, too, began with the apparition of an angel. Starting in 1820, while he was still an adolescent, Smith witnessed several apparitions. The most significant took place on the evening of September 21, 1823, while the youth was deep in prayer. A bright light filled his room, and an angel named Moroni (or Nephi) appeared to him. The angel revealed that a holy text engraved on golden plates was buried in a nearby hill, and that Smith must find them and translate them. The text was accompanied by two stones that would help him to translate; they were the *urim* and *thummim*, the same sacred stones Moses speaks of in the Bible, notably in the Book of Exodus.

Smith relates that the angel visited him for the next four years, always on the same date. And so on September 22, 1827, he went to the Hill Cumorah and found buried there a stone chest containing golden plates engraved with Egyptian characters, and two diamonds set in glass and mounted in silver bows, shaped much like eyeglasses. His mission was to translate the text and thus reveal the holy book of the new religion: the Book of Mormon.

According to the book, Moroni secreted the book in Hill Cumorah in the year A.D. 421. The text recounts the history of the first Americans. It speaks of three great nations, the Nephites, the Lamanites, and the Jaredites. Two were destroyed, but the Lamanites became the ancestors of American Indians. Jesus Christ had come to the American continent after His crucifixion, bringing his teachings to the indigenous people.

According to Mormon theology, Moroni is the other angel Smith speaks of in the Apocalypse, "flying in midair, having the everlasting gospel to preach unto them that dwell on the earth, to every nation and tribe and language and people."

On April 6, 1830, in Kirtland, Ohio, Joseph Smith founded the Church of Latter-Day Saints, claiming thus to reestablish the original church of Jesus Christ. He became its first president.

Joseph Smith and his believers, opposed to slavery, were chased from town to town in the South, and in 1839 he founded the town of Nauvoo in Illinois and served as its mayor. In January 1844, Smith announced his candidacy for president of the United States. But on June 27, 1844, Joseph and his brother Hyrum, who had both been jailed for destroying the presses of a newspaper which had written unfavorably about them, were murdered by an angry mob.

After their death came the exodus of Mormon pioneers to Utah, where they founded Salt Lake City in the Great Salt Lake Desert.

Today the church has eleven million members.

"A POOR, TORN HEART,
A TATTERED HEART"

EMILY DICKINSON (1830–1886)

A poor, torn heart, a tattered heart,
That sat it down to rest,
Nor noticed that the Ebbing Day
Flowed silver to the West,
Nor noticed Night did soft descend,
Nor Constellation burn,
Intent upon the vision
Of latitudes unknown.

The angels, happening that way
This dusty heart espied,
Tenderly took it up from toil
And carried it to God,
There—sandals for the Barefoot,
There—gathered from the gales,
Do the blue havens by the hand
Lead the wandering Sails.

O Saint Ange Gardien, faites-moi toujours marcher dans le chemin où croissent les lys de la pureté, afin que le regard de Dieu se repose sur mon âme avec amour!

(S. + C.)

BOUASSE-JEUNE   4047   12, PLACE St SULPICE, PARIS

Blessed guardian Angel, make me always walk the path where the lilies of purity grow, that God's gaze may fall upon my soul with love!

BIBLIOGRAPHY

Among the many books that have been written about angels, here are a few that were particularly helpful in compiling this album:

- *Anges et démons* (*Angels and Demons*), Rosa Giorgi, translated (from Italian to French) by Dominique Férault, Publisher: Hazan.

- Two titles by Philippe Olivier, published by De Vecchi: *Les Anges et les Archanges*; *Les Séraphims et les Chérubins* (*Angels and Archangels*; *Seraphim and Cherubim*).

- *Le Réveil des anges, messagers des peurs et des consolations* (*The Wakening of Angels, Messengers of Dread and Consolation*), Olivier Abel, Series: Collection Mutations, Publisher: Autrement.

- *Encyclopédie des anges* (*Encyclopedia of Angels*), Émilie Bonvin, Publisher: Éditions Exclusif.

- *La Légende des anges* (*The Legend of Angels*), Michel Serres, Publisher: Flammarion.

- *Traité des anges* (*Treatise on Angels*), Édouard Brasey, Publisher: Le Pré aux Clercs.

- *Les Anges et leur mission d'après les Pères de l'Église* (*Angels and Their Mission, According to the Fathers of the Church*), Jean Daniélou, Publisher: Chevetogne.

- *A Book of Angels*, Sophy Burnham, Publisher: Ballantine Books.